HAPPY BIRTHDAY TO US!

A note from our editor, Erik the Ed:

Welcome to this special birthday edition of the *Viking Express*. It's 1066, and that means the *Express* is 275 years old!

It goes all the way back to the AD 790s, when our Viking **ancestors** first arrived in Britain. They sailed across the stormy seas from their homeland in **Scandinavia**. At first, they just came to raid and steal things. But since then Viking families have settled in Britain and Ireland. We've changed British history.

To celebrate our 275th anniversary, we've put together a selection of our all-time favourite news stories. They are organized by subject, and you can find the dates beside each article. We hope you enjoy this look back at the past – and the present!

INSIDE...

Some words are shown in bold, **like this**. You can find out what they mean by looking in the glossary.

read on...

26 September 1066

Andrew Langley

Raintree is an imprint of Capstone Global Library Limited, a company incorporated in England and Wales having its registered office at 264 Banbury Road, Oxford, OX2 7DY – Registered company number: 6695582

www.raintree.co.uk
myorders@raintree.co.uk

Edited by Helen Cox Cannons
Designed by Philippa Jenkins
Original illustrations © Capstone Global Library Limited 2017
Illustrations on pages 1, 15 and 29 by Philippa Jenkins
Picture research by Eric Gohl
Production by Kathy McColley
Originated by Capstone Global Library Limited
Printed and bound in India

ISBN 978 1 4747 4211 5 (hardcover)
21 20 19 18 17
10 9 8 7 6 5 4 3 2 1

ISBN 978 1 4747 4212 2 (paperback)
22 21 20 19 18
10 9 8 7 6 5 4 3 2 1

British Library Cataloguing in Publication Data
A full catalogue record for this book is available from the British Library.

Acknowledgements
We would like to thank the following for permission to reproduce photographs: Alamy Stock Photo: Cindy Hopkins, 19 (top), imageBROKER, 4 (bottom), INTERFOTO, 18 (right), Jean Hall, 9, Jonathan Ball, 7, Kim Petersen, 4 (top), Panther Media GmbH, 18 (top left), Richard Peel, 5 (bottom), 10; Capstone: 5 (top, person), 6, 8 (all), 21 (top); Newscom: Arco Images G/picture alliance/ Therin-Weise, 13 (left), Danita Delimont Photography/Cindy Miller Hopkins, 14, Heritage Images/CM Dixon, 27 (all), Prisma/Album, 28 (bottom left), robertharding/David Lomax, 23 (top), World History Archive, 11; Shutterstock: Algol, 24 (ships), Allan Morrison, 12 (person), Dm_Cherry, cover (middle right), duchy, 25 (cliffs), Dudarev Mikhail, 25 (bottom, person), Elenarts, 24 (ship), Emjay Smith, 12 (cow), Eric Isselee, 28 (top right), Frank Bach, 22 (top), Good_mechanic, 19 (middle), Jennifer Westmoreland, 28 (top left), jps, 4 (middle), Kachalkina Veronika, cover (top left), 24 (person), Khosro, cover (bottom right), 20 (person), Marcin Perkowski, 20 (top, raven), Martin Prochazkacz, 24 (whale), melis, 26 (crowd), Nejron Photo, cover (middle left & top right), 16, 17, 21 (bottom), 25 (top, person), periscope, cover (bottom middle), 20 (bottom right, raven), Popova Valeriya, 13 (right), 26 (musicians), Rob Christiaans, 28 (bottom right), Roxana Bashyrova, 19 (bottom), Ryan Ladbrook, 20 (bottom left, raven), s_oleg, 25 (birds), soulofbeach, 26 (background), Sytilin Pavel, 18 (bottom left), tarake, 23 (bottom), trattieritratti, 5 (top, reeds), Vishnevskiy Vasily, cover (bottom left); SuperStock: Photononstop, 22 (bottom).

We would like to thank Dr Lesley Robinson for her invaluable help in the preparation of this book.

BIG NEWS WHERE'S ALF?

Somerset, January AD 878

King hides from Vikings

King Alfred, ruler of Wessex, is missing. He was forced to flee when his kingdom was invaded by the Great Army of the Vikings. But where has he gone?

Experts believe that he is hiding here, in the marshes of Somerset. He has a small band of soldiers, and has built a fort on a hill. The winter floods have turned the hill into an island. Locals call it Athelney, which means "island of the king". The Vikings do not dare attack him here. But how long can he hold out for?

WESSEX WIPEOUT!

Wiltshire, May AD 878

The Vikings suffered their biggest ever defeat in battle here at Edington in Wiltshire today. Our troops were hammered by a brand new English army. The army was led by King Alfred, who left his hideout in the marshes in an amazing comeback. Now we've been booted out of Wessex. It's a dark day for us **Danes**.

NORSE NORTH-EAST
Danelaw splits England

London, c. AD 886

The Vikings are here to stay. And we've got our own little corner of England. It's called the Danelaw.

Two leaders signed a historic **treaty** today. Alfred of Wessex and the Viking King Guthrum agreed to divide the country in two. The Vikings are in charge of eastern England. We can do what we like in the east, but must stop invading the western part.

"What's life like in the Danelaw?"

I asked a Norfolk farmer, who said:

"You Vikings have got a different language and different clothes from us. And you've got funny names. But we'll have to put up with it, I suppose."

Special correspondent Balder Sacoot reports

Where is the Danelaw? Take a map of England. Draw a line between London and Chester. The land to the west (left) of the line is ruled by the English and Welsh. The land to the east (right) is ruled by the Vikings. This is the Danelaw.

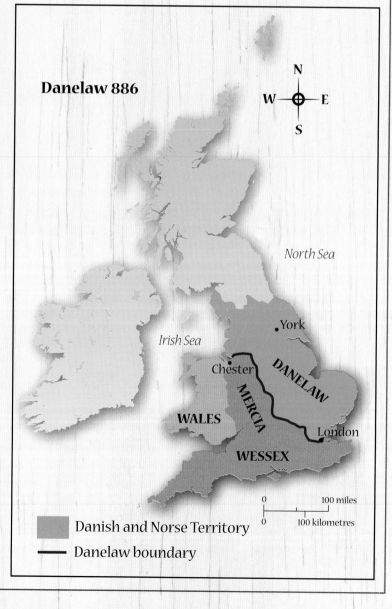

Danelaw 886

North Sea

Irish Sea

York

Chester

DANELAW

WALES

MERCIA

London

WESSEX

0   100 miles

0   100 kilometres

Danish and Norse Territory

—— Danelaw boundary

HAROLD v HARALD

Is this the end of the Vikings in Britain?

Our last great leader is dead

Yorkshire, 25 September 1066

Harald Hardrada of Norway had high hopes of conquering England when he landed in Yorkshire. But today he was killed in fighting at Stamford Bridge.

The battle ended in a great victory for the English army, led by another King Harold – Harold Godwinson of Wessex. Hearing of Hardrada's attack, he had marched north from London at top speed. Only a few Vikings survived, and they were soon chased back to their ships. We'll never conquer the whole of Britain now!

RELIGIOUS NEWS

THOR POINT

Know your Norse Gods

Saxons! Don't look dumb when the Vikings come calling. It's easy to get confused by our religion, with all its strange monsters and **myths**. So here's a guide to our main Viking Gods.

Odin

God of War. Odin is the most powerful of all. He has only one eye, and two ravens perch on his shoulders.

Thor

Son of Odin and God of Thunder and Lightning. Thor is strong and quick-tempered. He carries a huge hammer.

Frigg

Odin's wife and Goddess of childbirth. Frigg can see into the future.

Loki

Adopted son of Odin. The son of a giant, Loki is a liar and a trickster. His cunning helps the gods – and harms them too.

RELIGIOUS NEWS

IONA THE LONELY

Monks flee Scottish island

By our religious affairs correspondent, Simon Cowl

Inner Hebrides, AD 849

It's a tough time to be a monk. Their remote **monasteries** are prime targets for our Viking ships. Our raiders know they will find treasure as well as cattle and sheep.

The island of Iona, in the Inner Hebrides, has been hardest hit by raiders. Once home to Saint Columcille, the monastery here has suffered four savage Viking attacks since AD 795. Now the monks have given up. They are leaving Iona for good and going to Ireland. "We're getting out of here," said one of the monks. "And we're taking the bones of the great Columcille with us."

BUSINESS NEWS

BY GUM, WE'RE THE BIGGEST!

York grows into a world trade centre

York, c. AD 950

There's no doubt about it – York is now the biggest and busiest town in Britain. Its shops and markets are full of amazing items. Look at what you might find here:

- **silk cloth** from **Byzantium**
- **amber** from the **Baltic**
- **precious shells** from the Red Sea
- **wine** from Germany
- **walrus tusks** from Iceland

Norse traders bring in these goods from all over the world. But the Vikings of York are just as good at making things. Craft workers in the narrow streets turn out anything from stone pots and wooden cups to leather shoes, helmets and glass. Jewellers make beautiful **ornaments** from gold and silver and black **jet**.

BUSINESS NEWS

PAY UP—OR ELSE!

Viking money expert Bjorn Loaded explains how Danegeld works

Essex, AD 992

Danegeld: it's simple. We're Vikings, and Vikings are **Danes**. We'll rob you and burn your homes unless you give us lots of gold (or geld – that's why it's called Danegeld, geddit?).

Everybody's happy. You get to keep your property safe. We get to keep the gold. This year it's going to cost King Ethelred 22,000 pounds of gold and silver to stay safe. Not bad for a bit of peace, is it?

IT'S A SNIP!
Fed up with a purse full of little coins?
Why not switch to hacksilver?

Instead of coins, just carry one big lump of hacksilver when you go shopping. If you want to pay for something, simply hack a bit off.

FARMING NEWS

JOBS FOR THE GIRLS

Women do most farm work

Ulster, c. AD 850

There's always a lot to do on a Viking farm. Soil has to be ploughed, crops sown and harvested, cattle fed and hay gathered in. Everyone in the family, from grannies to little kids, has to work.

But Viking men get restless. They often take long trips away in their boats. They go fishing or trading. And many of them go raiding up and down the coast. So who does all the hard work then?

"We do, of course!"

says Irish farmer, Frigga Digger.

"My husband comes back to help harvest, but for most of the year I'm in charge. Without women, no food would get grown at all."

FARMING NEWS

MEAT AND HEAT

What's winter like in a longhouse? Farm reporter Cnut Cowpat went to find out

Northumbria, c. AD 900

Snow lies thick on the ground. A freezing wind whistles off the North Sea. But inside Hamar's longhouse it's all snug and warm.

Hamar and his farming family sit on benches around a fire that burns on stones in the middle of the floor. They live at one end of the long, narrow house. At the other end is the pen for the cattle. They stay inside all winter to keep them safe from thieves.

It's pretty smelly in the longhouse. The smoke from the fire mixes with the pong from the cattle. But Hamar doesn't mind. "Cows give out a lot of heat," says Hamar, "so they make us even warmer!"

A DAY IN THE LIFE

This week...
THE BOAT BUILDER

Dublin, 1055

"You can't beat a Viking longship,"

says Dermot O'Poopdeck.

"They're the fastest, the strongest and the most beautiful boats on the sea."

And he should know. He builds them.

Each morning, Dermot walks to the shipyard in Dublin harbour. A longship takes many weeks to make. Here's how he goes about it:

· He lays the keel. This is a long, straight piece of oak, which is the backbone of the ship. Curved posts are fixed at each end with wooden pegs.

· He builds the **hull** (the body of the ship) on top of the keel by nailing oak planks, which overlap each other.

· He makes the oak frame inside the hull, with a hole for the mast to slot into.

· He fills tiny gaps in the planks with moss and wool. This stops the water from getting in.

The ship's ready to go!

LETTERS TO THE EDITOR

Readers tell the Viking Express what they *really* think

Tomorrow you'll be yesterday

You Vikings think you're all very fierce and frightening. You come over here and win a few battles and build a few towns. You even give them Viking names. But you won't last. In 1,000 years' time nobody will remember anything about you at all.

Yours sincerely,
DONALD THE DIMWIT

York, AD 792

Vikings smell better

I came to Britain from Denmark. The first thing I noticed was how stinky and untidy the British people are. They never seem to wash. We Vikings comb our hair every day – and have a bath once a week.

Yours sincerely,
ERIK SHOWERGEL

Derby, AD 950

Watch out!

Why is everyone so rude about the Vikings? Some of them are a bit bloodthirsty, but the rest came in peace. All they wanted was land where they could settle and bring up their children. If you think they're bad, just wait. I've heard rumours that the Normans are planning to invade us next!

Yours, quivering in my boots,
EDA BIGKNEES

London, 1066

CELEB NEWS

First with the latest about people who matter

EGIL SAVES HIS SKIN

East Anglia, 1000

Egil Uglyskull is famous for two reasons – he's a great poet and a savage warrior. And we've seen both sides of him since he arrived here from Iceland.

Egil has killed a lot of people, mostly when he flies into a rage. Then he boasted that he would kill King Erik Bloodaxe. It's no surprise that King Erik locked him up and sentenced him to death.

When Egil calmed down, he knew there was only one way to stay alive. He wrote a long poem about Erik, saying how wonderful and wise he was. The king was so amazed that he forgave Egil and let him go free.

CELEB NEWS

QUEEN OF MYSTERY

East Anglia, 1000

Who is Sigrid the **Haughty**? Mystery surrounds the glamorous new queen of England. Since she married King Sweyn Forkbeard, she has rarely been seen out in public.

Why is she called Sigrid the Haughty? She is known to be very beautiful, and her first husband was also a king – Erik the Victorious of Sweden. After he died, many other men wanted to marry her, but she **rejected** them. She even had two of them burned to death. Sweyn Forkbeard must be something special!

GREAT EXPLORER COMES TO WESSEX

Hampshire, AD 890

King Alfred had a surprise visitor today – the famous **seafarer** Ottar of Heligoland. Ottar told the king about his amazing voyages into the unknown. He reached the White Sea, a long way north of Norway. It was a cold and icy wasteland, he said. The only living things there were the tough tribe of Finns, and a lot of whales and walruses.

FASHION HIGHLIGHTS

By Olav Olay

C. AD **950**

TAKE IT WITH YOU
and look smart too!

Viking women have to carry all sorts of things wherever they go: keys, combs, needle cases, little knives. Where do you put them all? The latest answer is … chains! Everyone wears a brooch or two for fastening their dresses and aprons. Simply fix wire chains to your brooches, and hang all your little bits on them. This leaves your hands free to do other things!

VIKING BLING

If you've got it, show it off! Gold is no good when it's hidden away in a box. That's why wealthy Vikings like to wear gold jewellery when they can. A stunning example is this armband. It was made in York from three woven strands of gold.

LOOK RIGHT, DRESS TIGHT

Bye bye, baggy trousers. Today's man is wearing them skin-tight. In fact, some Viking warriors have such tight trousers they have trouble taking them off!

HANDY HINTS

Your questions answered by Harald the Handyman

Q: I'm in a hurry to cook a meal. How can I light a fire? Rubbing sticks together is just too slow.

A: *Stick rubbing is so Stone Age! Modern folk, like us Vikings, use a Strike-a-light. This is a curved piece of iron with a piece of steel on it. Hit the steel with a piece of* **flint** *and – bingo! – you get a spark. Catch this in a piece of cloth, blow gently and you'll soon have a flame.*

Q: I keep falling off my horse. What can I do about it?

A: *Poor you! But it's hard to stay on a horse if your feet are waving about. Our Viking friends brought over a jolly useful invention called a stirrup. You have two of these, one each side, attached to the saddle. Stick your feet in your stirrups and you'll never fall off again.*

Q: I'm building a new **longship**, and I want to make it look really scary. What's the best way?

A: *Get a chunk of wood and carve a great big dragon's head, with huge staring eyes and snarling jaws. Then fix it on a post on the prow (front) of the ship. That should be frightening enough!*

Q: How can I learn to read runes?

A: *With a bit of hard work! Though it's not too hard. We Vikings use a simple set of marks called runes for writing down words. There are only 16 characters, each with a different sound. But there's a catch: some runes have more than one sound. You can read more tips in* Runing and Scoring *by Wayne Runey (Manchester Press, 5 pounds of gold).*

TRAVEL NEWS

SNOW PROBLEM

We Vikings are used to snow and ice. Cold weather doesn't keep us at home. So in winter we can easily travel about the countryside – even on rivers. How do we do it?

♦ On skates
Vikings make ice skates from the leg bones of cattle. Then we tie them to our feet with leather laces.

♦ On sledges
Big sledges, made of oak or pine, can carry heavier loads than an ordinary cart can.

♦ On skis
Viking hunters whizz through forests on wide skis made of birchwood, with leather straps.

RAVEN MAD!

Shetland, AD 860

Intrepid sailor Floki never gets lost at sea – thanks to his three ravens. "I was sailing from Shetland to Iceland, and didn't know the way," he explained.

"When I released the first raven, it flew back to Shetland. When I released the second, it saw no land, and returned to the ship. Later, I let the third raven go. It flew straight ahead. And I followed, because I knew it had seen Iceland."

TRAVEL NEWS

OVER THE OCEAN
Leif finds a brand new world

North America, c. 1000

Nothing stops Vikings from exploring. First we came to Britain and Ireland. Then it was Iceland, then Greenland. Today we have news of an even more amazing voyage that took **Norsemen** all the way to the other side of the world!

Led by Leif Ericsson, a boatload of sailors landed on an unknown land. They found green fields, fresh water, and plenty of fish and game to eat. Leif calls it Vinland. It seems a perfect place to settle. There's room for an awful lot of people there!

Leif Ericsson's route to Vinland

HOMES FOR SALE

Wexford, Ireland
Rare chance to buy a **longphort**!

Once used by Viking settlers as a camp or **settlement** to keep ships, this longphort has been lovingly **restored**. The site on the banks of the River Slaney is ideal for a **seafarer**. There's a landing place for boats and a sturdy timber house. And the whole place is surrounded by a tall fence to keep your enemies out.

Price: 500 pounds of gold

Jarlshof, Shetland
Stonebuilt farmhouse with all mod cons.

This island home boasts a cosy kitchen, living room and animal shed. It also has two doors, one on each side of the house. Just use the door that faces away from the wind and you won't have any nasty draughts. Other buildings include a bathhouse, **blacksmith's** workshop and a kiln for drying corn.

Price: one year's supply of fish

HOMES FOR SALE

Midlothian, Scotland

Worried about Viking raiders? You'll be safe and snug inside this **souterrain** (underground house).

Made of solid rock, this souterrain is the perfect hideaway. The earth walls are stylishly lined with stone, and the ceilings with wood. There's plenty of storage space, plus a secret chamber with a hidden door.

Price: 200 sheep

York, England

Neat little house in the centre of bustling city.

The walls of this house are made of wattle – wood strips woven between upright posts. The roof is eco-friendly straw – the best for keeping heat indoors. The house has one compact room, with a stone fireplace and raised sleeping platforms on either side.

Price: 5,000 silver pennies

FOOD AND DRINK

FRIGHTFUL FOOD: Part 1
Special report on whale hunting

Whale meat again

Finn Fishbone watches a whale hunt

Northumbria, c. 1000

The old sailor watched the ships move out to sea. He said:

"They must be mad. You wouldn't catch me out there."

Whale hunting is very dangerous. The ships were being tossed about by huge waves. Then they turned and headed back again in a line.

I could just see a huge, dark shape swimming in front of them. It was a whale!

Slowly, the rowers drove the whale in towards the shore. Soon it was stranded on the beach. Hunters raced to meet it. They carried bows, arrows and spears. That whale will provide a lot of meat for the winter.

FOOD AND DRINK

FRIGHTFUL FOOD: Part 2
You've got to be yolking

Gitte Meoutofhere goes in search of seabird eggs

Orkney, c. AD **980**

Help! I'm dangling from a rope – halfway down a cliff!

Far below is the sea, with nasty jagged rocks sticking out. I've got a little bag slung over my shoulder. My job is to collect gulls' eggs. The folk round here love to eat them. I find a nest and take out three eggs. The birds are angry and they scream around my head. I don't like this! Pull me up, now.

Please?

Today's recipe

Beef boiled in a pit full of hot stones

Ingredients:
Beef, cut into pieces
Water
Herbs, if you can find any

Method:
Dig a pit and line it with wood. Put the meat into the pit. Pour water over the meat and herbs (optional). Now drop in some very hot stones from the fire. Cook for an hour, adding more hot stones to keep it boiling.

ARTS AND ENTERTAINMENT

JESTER MINUTE!
Last night's big gig

Reviewed by Britt Popp

London, AD 899

Crowds packed into the Great Hall next to the River Thames last night. And no wonder – people had come to hear the very best in Viking music.

First up were the Jesters. Most of their songs were very rude and very funny. They were backed by bone pipes and brass horns. The beat of the drums and iron rattles soon got the crowd dancing. After this, the **Skalds** (poets) came on to sing about heroes and monsters. Their music, played on harps and lyres, was much gentler.

But a lot of people don't like Viking music. One foreign visitor told me, "I've never heard such ugly songs. That growling sound from their throats reminds me of dogs howling!" Another said their singing sounded like a cart rolling downhill.

ARTS AND ENTERTAINMENT

SMALL IS BEAUTIFUL
The Pitney Brooch

Somerset, 1065

Experts in the jewellery world have been stunned by the Pitney brooch. It's tiny – no bigger than a walnut. But it's also a great work of art. It is the latest of many amazing products from the Viking craftworkers of England.

The brooch is made of copper and covered with a thin layer of gold. It shows a long, thin dragon, which is coiled in the shape of a heart. The dragon is being attacked by a snake with big, gleaming eyes. It will make the perfect Christmas present for some lucky person!

REMEMBERING THE RAID

Lindisfarne, c. AD 820

Vikings first hit these shores back in AD 793. Our raiders brought terror to Lindisfarne Island and destroyed its **Christian monastery**. Now, that vital moment is remembered in a stunning new sculpture on the island. Carved into a gravestone are the figures of warriors armed with swords and axes (that's us!). On the other side are a sun and moon, with people praying.

FOR SALE

HOUSEHOLD

Twenty large balls of wool
The best – it comes from Herdwick sheep in Cumbria. Ideal for weaving into cloth.

Thor's hammer pendant
Lucky charm, which could make you as strong as the god himself!

Hnefatafl
Crazy name, crazy game! As played by the Vikings. Complete with board and pieces in its original box.

Comb and case
Keep your hair tidy with this lovely comb carved from bone.

Load of mixed fish
All sorts, including cod and herring. Landed today. Please buy soon or our neighbours will complain of the smell.

FARM AND GARDEN

Wooden cart
Four wheels, all in top condition. Plus harness for two horses thrown in free.

Single stirrup
The other was lost. Suitable for one-legged rider.

Iron battle axe
As new. Never used. Owner ran away from battle.

Apple trees for sale
Grow your own apples, just like the gods eat. Ready for planting now.

PETS AND FARM ANIMALS

Ship's cat
Good mouse catcher. Well used to **longship** voyages.

Viking bull
Brought all the way from Norway. Has enormous horns, just right for helmets.

Please, give a home to Rakki
Rakki the Reindeer Dog is great for herding reindeer. But he is also an ideal pet. He loves children and is a fine guard dog.

Colony of bees
Have your very own honey supply. They've set up home in our roof. Buyer collects.

SERVICES

Hole in your sail?
We'll mend it for you while you wait!
Nanna's **Norse** Knitters.

What Wattle of Watford
Come to us for all your building supplies. Clay, straw, stone and – of course – lots of wattle. Free delivery.

Sagas for You!
We'll write a **saga** and make you the hero, telling of all your fantastic adventures. Go down in history – even if you're very boring.
Contact: *Sagas for You, Sutton Hoo, Suffolk*

TIMELINE

AD 700

793
Viking raiders attack the **Christian monastery** on the island of Lindisfarne

795
First Viking raids take place on the coasts of Ireland

806
Vikings burn the abbey on the island of Iona, Scotland

849
Monks abandon their monastery on the island of Iona after repeated raids

841
Vikings build their first **settlements** in Dublin, Ireland

c. 835
Vikings begin to settle in Scotland

c. 860
The explorer Floki uses ravens to help him find his way to Iceland

865
The Danish Great Army lands in East Anglia

874
Vikings begin to settle in Iceland

878
Alfred the Great defeats the **Danes** at the Battle of Edington

c. 950
York becomes the most important Viking town in England. Erik Bloodaxe rules East Anglia.

886
The leaders of Wessex and the Danes split England in two. Viking area of land in the east is called the Danelaw.

992
King Ethelred pays "Danegeld" to the Vikings to stop them attacking him

AD 1000

c. 1000
Sigrid the **Haughty** marries Sweyn Forkbeard

1000
Viking sailors, led by Leif Ericsson, land on the coast of America

1013
Sweyn Forkbeard of Denmark conquers England

1066
Harold of Wessex defeats Harald Hardrada at the Battle of Stamford Bridge

c. 1065
The Pitney Brooch is made

1055
Evidence shows that **longships** were being built in Dublin

GLOSSARY

amber yellow or brown hardened tree sap used to make jewellery

ancestor person we are descended from (such as a mother or a great-great-grandfather)

Baltic area of land near the Baltic Sea, in the eastern Atlantic Ocean

Byzantium ancient Greek city, founded in the 7th century BC

Christian someone who follows the religion that teaches about the life of Jesus Christ

Dane one of the Viking invaders of Britain during the 9th to 11th centuries

flint very hard and shiny type of stone, which sparks when struck with steel

hacksilver small chunk of silver cut from a larger piece and used as money

haughty proud and vain

hnefatafl Viking game, in which players move pieces on a board marked in squares (like chess)

hull main body of a ship

jet hard, black coal that can be made into jewellery when carefully polished

longphort early Viking camp or settlement where ships could easily be landed and kept

longship narrow and fast-moving vessel used by the Vikings

monastery religious centre where monks live and work

myth traditional story about the beginnings of a country or people, usually filled with gods, monsters and other supernatural beings

Norse Norwegian from Norway or Scandinavian from Iceland and Sweden during ancient times

pendant piece of jewellery that hangs from a necklace

restore when something is put back into its original condition

saga story told or sung from person to person about ancient Viking times, mixing historical facts and legends

Scandinavia region of Northern Europe which contains the modern countries of Denmark, Sweden, Norway, Finland and Iceland

seafarer person who regularly travels at sea

settlement place where people settle and make their home

silk smooth, shiny fabric made from fibres produced by silkworms

Skald ancient Norse poet or singer

souterrain underground shelter using caves or tunnels dug into soil

treaty agreement between two leaders or states

FIND OUT MORE

There's a lot more to learn about the Vikings in Britain and Ireland – and about their other amazing travels around the world. New discoveries are being made all the time. Read about them in books or online, or visit some of the hundreds of great websites or museum exhibits around the country. Here's just a tiny selection to get you started.

BOOKS

Everything Vikings, Nadia Higgins (National Geographic Kids, 2015)

The Viking and Anglo-Saxon Struggle for England (Early British History), Claire Throp (Raintree, 2015)

The Vikings (Britain in the Past), Moira Butterfield (Franklin Watts, 2015)

The Vikings (History Hunters), Louise Spilsbury (Raintree, 2016)

Vicious Vikings (Horrible Histories), Terry Deary and Martin Brown (Scholastic, 2016)

WEBSITES

www.bbc.co.uk/education/topics/ztyr9j6

This BBC website has information on the Vikings, including videos, animations and lots more.

www.ngkids.co.uk/history/10-facts-about-the-vikings

This National Geographic site gives you ten fascinating facts that you didn't know about the Vikings!

primaryhomeworkhelp.co.uk/vikings.html

This site gives lots of information about Viking life in Britain, including more about the Danelaw and Viking houses and settlements.

PLACES TO VISIT

Here are a few of the many great Viking sites and museums you can visit. Is there one near you?

Ancient Technology Centre
Cranborne, BH21 5RP
See a reconstruction of a Viking longhouse.

British Museum
London, WC1B 3DG
The Viking section here has treasures, weapons and a lot more.

House of Manannan
Peel, Isle of Man, IM5 1TA
Find out what life was like on a Viking longship or in a longhouse.

Jorvik Viking Centre
York, YO1 9WT
This exciting museum is built on the site of Viking Age York.

National Museum of Ireland
Dublin 2, Ireland
You can see a display of Viking objects dug up near Dublin.

National Museum of Scotland
Edinburgh, EH1 1JF
This has many Viking exhibits, including swords, brooches, combs, plus a model of a longship.

INDEX